THE IRAN-IRAQ WAR

Saddam Hussein's Attack in the Middle East

Written by Corentin de Favereau
Translated by Carly Probert

History | 50MINUTES.com

THE IRAN-IRAQ WAR

KEY INFORMATION

- **When:** 22 September 1980 – 20 August 1988
- **Where:** In Iran and Iraq
- **Context:** The Islamic revolution in Iran and the territorial expansion policy in Iraq
- **Belligerents:** The Islamic Republic of Iran against the Republic of Iraq
- **Commanders and leaders:**
    - Ruhollah Musavi Khomeini, Supreme Leader of the Islamic Republic of Iran (1902-1989)
    - Saddam Hussein, president of Iraq (1937-2006)
- **Outcome:** Status quo
- **Victims:**
    - Iranian camp: between 220 000 and 400 000 deaths
    - Iraqi camp: between 200 000 and 500 000 deaths

INTRODUCTION

As part of an ancient struggle between Iran and Iraq, the war of 1980-1988 (known in Iran as the "Sacred Defense") was one of the deadliest conflict since 1945, as well as the longest. While President Saddam Hussein wanted to make his Republic of Iraq a powerful force in the region, Ayatollah Ruhollah Musavi Khomeini meanwhile planned to export his Islamic Revolution beyond the borders of Iran and extend it to the Iraqis. With the pretext of multiple provocations around their border, Saddam Hussein launched his troops to conquer the Shatt al-Arab (Middle Eastern river), and proclaimed their complete domination over this area on 22 September 1980. A war erupted that people hoped would be very short, but it was soon slowed down and took the form of a war of attrition. Thus, after eight years of fierce fighting and a price of several hundred thousand deaths on both sides, neither of these two great powers of the Gulf could claim victory. However, this conflict, which was absurd in many ways, generated dreadful bloodshed and culminated in a disastrous economic situation for the two warring countries, strengthened the hold of the two men in their respective countries and ensured their power.

GOOD TO KNOW

An ayatollah ("sign of God") is an honorary title awarded to the highest Shiite dignitaries. The ayatollahs are considered experts of Islam. They teach in Islamic schools and claim to be descendants of the Prophet Muhammad (570-632), through his son-in-law, Ali (1st century A.D.).

POLITICAL AND SOCIAL CONTEXT

THE ARAB RIVER

On 22 September 1980, Saddam Hussein declared war on Iran, using the territorial disagreement that had plagued relations between the two neighbors for several years as an excuse to do so. For him, it was a case of asserting his right over territories that were legitimately Iraqi, but which had been amputated from Iraq five years earlier by a treaty with Iran.

Following the First World War (1914-1918) and the collapse of the Ottoman Empire (1922), which then extended over much of the Middle East, the borders of the region had been fully redrawn, according to the interests of the victorious Western powers, namely France and Britain. However, throughout the 20th century, this artificial division was questioned extensively. In the Gulf, the agreement of Algiers from 1975 – in which Iran continued to provide military aid to Iraqi Kurds in exchange for recognition of the Iraq border of the Shatt al-Arab River – was supposed to end territorial tensions that animated the two countries. Yet, the stakes were high with regards to the Shatt al-Arab, literally the "Rivers of the Arabs", because it connected the oil areas of both countries. Thus, despite the agreement between the two neighbors, the strategic importance of this area did not fail to cause many provocations and confrontations until the rejection of the treaty by Saddam Hussein on 17 September 1980, and the conquest of the disputed territories five days later.

AN IDEOLOGICAL POWDER KEG

Along with the territorial tensions that divided them, Iran and Iraq were also opposed ideologically. The war was actually triggered in the context of the opposition of the Shiites from Iraq, supported by Iran, to the regime of Saddam Hussein. This support caused Hussein to fear that the Islamic revolution that occurred in Iran the previous year might contaminate his country.

For many months, Iran faced a popular uprising animated from France by Ayatollah Ruhollah Musavi Khomeini who was in exile therein. The people protested against the increasingly authoritarian regime of the Shah (title of the Iranian emperors) and the forced "Western" modernization, known as the "White Revolution" (1963). Thus, on 16 January 1979, the pressure became too strong and the Shah decided to leave Iran to take refuge in the United States.

Poster of the Iranian revolution showing the Shah taking refuge in the United States, 1979.

Four days later, Ruhollah Musavi Khomeini, empowered by his broad popular support, returned triumphant to Tehran. After ensuring the neutrality of the armed forces, the Ayatollah declared the end of the monarchy on 11 February and set up a provisional government. The fundamentalist clergy operating under the name of the "Revolutionary Guard" then organized the systematic taking of control of key positions in the administration and conducted the extermination of figures from the old regime and opponents of any kind. Finally, following a referendum held on 1 April 1979, an Islamic republic was established, at the head of which Ruhollah Musavi Khomeini became the supreme leader.

Destruction of a statue of the Shah Mohammad Reza Pahlavi, February 1979.

However, he very quickly expressed his ambition to export his Islamic revolution and believed himself to be invested in the sacred mission to gather all Shiites around Iran, following a radical and fundamentalist reform of the existing regimes. To facilitate his goal, the Ayatollah further intended to capitalize on the anti-Arab and anti-Iraqi religious feeling that had been rooted in Persia for centuries. Thus, for Iraq, which held the majority of Shiite Arabs, the threat was now significant and very real.

DID YOU KNOW?

Persia was the name given to Iran until 1934, which was gradually abandoned after the advent of the Pahlavi dynasty in 1925. Originally, the Persians were a people from southwestern Iran. These gave rise to two vast empires, the Achaemenids, from the 6th century to the 4th century B.C., and the Sassanids, from the 3rd to the 7th century A.D. Today, Iranians speak Farsi (a Persian language) and are influenced by their own Persian culture, forged through the tumult of its long history.

GOOD TO KNOW

Islam is divided into two main currents:

- Firstly, Sunnism, which includes more than 80% of Muslims in the world;
- The other is Shiism, with about 10-15% of the world's Muslims, which constitutes 90% of the

Iranian population.

The Shiites define themselves as the *chi'at 'Ali* (meaning "party of Ali"). They attributed to Ali a role close to that of the prophet himself. According to them, he and his direct descendants, the Imams and the Ayatollah, were the only ones who could take on the spiritual direction of the community. Thus, while the Sunnis agree only to consider the Imams as the leaders of communal prayer, the Shiites regard them as the only guarantors of spiritual and secular authority.

In addition, these two currents differ in their approach to sacred texts. Indeed, the Sunnis, beside their classical interpretation of the Koran as a pillar of their doctrine, took into account the Sunnah, which represents Muhammad's course of action.

However, Iraq also holds an ideological interest in the conflict. In the same spirit of universality, Saddam Hussein intended to arabize the entire Gulf, advocating the unity of a modern, borderless Arab state and defending against the religious radicalism of the Persian archenemy. Thus, in his speeches, he introduced his fight as a continuity of the Hegira, a conquest during which the Arabs, defeating the Persians, managed to impose Islam. This way, he did not fail to recall the legitimacy of the Iraqis over Islam at the expense of Iranians, who were Persians, and were only converted to Islam later on.

Therefore, tensions between the two neighbors took a religious form, one wishing for the renaissance of Arabism and the other of Islamism.

BECOMING THE LEADING POWER IN THE GULF

Finally, under the cover of these complex ideological and cultural conflicts, the two nations also waged this merciless war for incredibly banal reasons, in comparison to history: money and power. Saddam Hussein and Ayatollah Ruhollah Musavi Khomeini were indeed sitting on huge reserves of good quality oil and which was extremely easy to extract. At the time, the two countries alone produced 10% of the world's oil. Thus, the one who could control the production of this black gold in the Gulf would be endowed with tremendous power, and would be able to influence the course of the global economy.

In Saddam Hussein's mind, this oil would allow him to have Iraq play a part in the play of the Western powers. Given the disruption of the Arab regional balance because of Syria's implication in the Lebanese civil war and the diplomatic estrangement of Egypt since its recognition of Israel in 1979, Saddam Hussein hoped to take advantage of a victory against Iran to rise to the top of Arab powers. On the other side of the Shatt al-Arab, the oil money would be used to finance campaigns to spread the Islamic Revolution of Ayatollah Ruhollah Musavi Khomeini.

COMMANDERS AND LEADERS

RUHOLLAH MUSAVI KHOMEINI, SUPREME LEADER OF THE ISLAMIC REPUBLIC OF IRAN

Ruhollah Musavi Khomeini, 1979.

Born in Khomein (Iranian city) in September 1902, Ruhollah Musavi Khomeini soon began theological training delivered by Professor Abdul Karin Hairi-Yazdi (1859-1937) in Arak. In 1922, as the professor left to teach at Qom, Ruhollah Musavi Khomeini decided to follow him. Three years later, he obtained his graduate degree in Sharia, and ethnic and spiritual philosophy.

Becoming a professor of theology, he rose to the position of Ayatollah in the fifties. At that time, he adopted a position that was increasingly opposed to the Shah's regime and pro-tested against the White Revolution aiming to modernize Iranian society. This challenge led to him being imprisoned in 1963. The following year, after his release prompted by pressure from the street and the clergy, he resumed his activism against the regime and was forced to flee to Turkey and then to Iraq where he was radicalized even further. Initially tolerated, his fight then became too pro-Shiite, so much so that Saddam Hussein decided to expel Ruhollah Musavi Khomeini, who moved to Neauphle-le-Château, France, in 1978.

His exile paradoxically reinforced his influence. His speeches were recorded on tape so that he could reach more people directly and thus lead his revolution from a distance. Popular pressure from the opponents had become too strong, so the Shah left Iran in January 1979, thus leaving room for Ruhollah Musavi Khomeini, who made a triumphant return to Tehran a few days later. Khomeini then proceeded with a referendum to elect a prime minister and announced the founding of the Islamic Republic of Iran on 1 April. He was appointed Supreme Leader.

On 4 November 1979, Islamic students took 52 U.S. diplomats hostage in order to obtain the extradition of the Shah, then in Washington. This attack, supported by the Ayatollah, truly launched the era of Khomeini, but above all signaled a turning point in international relations between the U.S. and Iran, which was previously an ally of the West.

Ruhollah Musavi Khomeini then showed his desire to extend the principles of the Islamic revolution to the entire Shiite world. This project raised the fears of Saddam Hussein of a Shiite revolt in Iraq, so he decided to invade Iran in 1980.

Poster of the Islamic Republic against Saddam Hussein's regime.

After an initially triumphant campaign of the Iraqi army, Ruhollah Musavi Khomeini was able to re-mobilize his troops and stop the invasion. Indeed, this attack allowed for the Ayatollah to silence this opposition by diverting it towards the enemy and to mobilize his troops by reviving a

Persian nationalist sentiment.

Convinced that the war against the Arab enemy was a gift from God, he refused all proposals for a cease-fire, an attitude which gradually transformed Iran's image as a victim to that of an invader. After eight years of war and more direct military intervention from the United States, the Ayatollah agreed to accept the UN resolution aimed at ending the war, rather than see his Islamic regime disintegrate.

Ruhollah Musavi Khomeini died in June 1989, leaving behind a country that was untouched, but economically devastated.

SADDAM HUSSEIN, PRESIDENT OF IRAQ

Saddam Hussein, 1979.

Saddam Hussein was born in A-Awja in Iraq on 28 April 1937. In 1955, he went to Baghdad to complete his education and integrated the Baath Party, which sought the unity of the

Arab nation beyond borders. Following his involvement in the attempted assassination of Prime Minister Abdul Karim Qasim (1914-1963) in 1959, Saddam Hussein fled to Syria and then to Egypt. When the Baath Party took power in 1963, he decided to return to Iraq. However, after a few months, Saddam Hussein's party was ousted by General Abdel Salam Aref (1921-1966). He was then sent to prison, but would escape a few years later. He then took part in the victorious revolution of 17 July 1968. His influence in the party became increasingly unavoidable. Thus, in 1979, the 11th anniversary of the revolution, Saddam Hussein took the supreme power and became president. In the process, he decided, the following year, to declare war on Iran, which he feared would extend the Islamic revolution to the Iraqi Shiites.

After a quick and victorious campaign, he announced the annexation of Khuzestan, a region of Iran with an Arab minority, where the land was rich in oil. However, the nationalist surge of the Iranians enabled them to stop the Iraqi incursions and caused the stagnation of the conflict. The bombing of oil interests by Iran and the continuation of the Iraqi fighting force forced Iraq to seek help from the Allied powers. By posing as a defender of the Arabs, Saddam Hussein ensured the support of other powers in the Gulf. Also, his gaze turned to the West and the USSR. By proposing peace talks that were rejected by Iran each time, Saddam Hussein was transforming his image from aggressor to victim. This reversal allowed foreign powers to justify their support for Iraq to the public opinion, until the revelations of Iraq's continued reliance on chemical weapons – weapons that he would also use against his own people.

Two years after the end of the war, in 1990, Saddam Hussein, eager to revive the economy of his country, tried to invade Kuwait and get hold of its oil. However, following this invasion, the United States of President George H.W. Bush (born 1924) led an international coalition and decided to launch a military intervention in January 1991 against Iraq. The attempts of Saddam Hussein turned into a fiasco and resulted in Iraq being marginalized in the international community.

Following the attacks of 11 September 2001 and the war against terrorism waged by the United States, it decided to overthrow Saddam Hussein under the pretext of the presence of weapons of mass destruction on his territory. This war, led by George Bush Jr. (born in 1946), would lead to the destruction of Saddam Hussein's regime and his execution on 30 December 2006.

ANALYSIS OF THE WAR

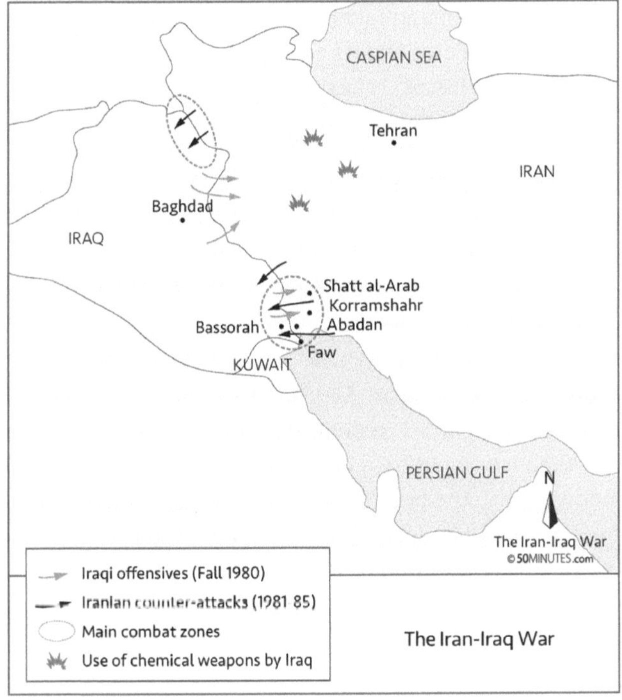

The Iran-Iraq War

After days of provocation and confrontation between Iran and Iraq around the demarcation of their common border, Saddam Hussein, who expected a military weakening of his Persian enemy, crossed the border on 10 September 1980. Iran refused any diplomatic discussions with Iraq, destroying all hope of a peaceful solution to the conflict at the same time.

The military solution seemed even more inescapable when, on 22 September, Iraq launched a surprise aerial attack on the Iranian Air Force and its economic interests. In the process, Saddam Hussein repealed the treaty that established the boundaries of the two countries and proclaimed his full sovereignty over the Shatt al-Arab. The two nations then engaged in a conflict that can be divided into eight distinct phases.

PHASE 1: A LIGHTNING WAR (SEPTEMBER 1980-WINTER 1981)

Upon starting the war, Saddam Hussein was convinced of his broad military superiority, which led him to think that the war would be quick and limited. Iraq was indeed endowed with the best Western and Soviet military equipment and had nearly 190 000 well-trained men. In addition, he relied on the purges operated by Ruhollah Musavi Khomeini from within his army, as he wanted to make a clean sweep of the Shah's regime. However, in doing so, he decapitated all of his armed force and significantly reduced its responsiveness. Thus, the first months of war justified Hussein's optimism: Iraq invaded Iran without major difficulty. But, on 28 September, the UN required the cessation of the fighting, to which Iraq responded that it would stop, if Iran recognized its domination over the Shatt al-Arab. However, Iran refused and bombarded the economic interests of Iraq. In mid-November, Iraq took the strategic city of Khorramshahr (Iranian port city) and besieged Abadan.

Before the winter truce, he occupied 25 900 km² of south and central Iran.

Battle of Khorramshahr (Iran), from 22 September to 10 November 1980.

PHASE 2: THE DEAD-END (APRIL 1981-MARCH 1982)

The attack on Iraq did not have the desired effect for Saddam Hussein, who had hoped to destabilize the Iranian government. On the contrary, the offensive galvanized the Iranian people, who, exalted by the nationalist speeches of Ruhollah Musavi Khomeini, engaged heavily in the conflict. Saddam Hussein had to revise his plans for quick success. Between December 1980 and December 1981, the positions did not change and the Iraqis were even forced to lift the siege on Abadan.

PHASE 3: RESPONSE AND STUBBORNNESS (MARCH 1982-JUNE 1982)

After breaking the siege of Abadan, Iran re-routed the Iraqi army and re-took, from March 1982, the majority of the territories lost to the center of the country. On 24 May, the city of Khorramshahr fell into Iranian hands. Following these successive failures, the thousands of prisoners taken by the enemy and the devastating effect of these events on morale, Iraq announced a cease-fire on 9 June. However, Tehran refused and decided to march on Baghdad. This stubbornness of Iran restored the image of Saddam Hussein, who appeared more and more like the victim. This rehabilitation within the international community and the progress of the Iranian army then promoted the enhancement of logistical and military support from the Western countries to Iraq.

PHASE 4: FAILURE OF THE RAMADAN OPERATION (JULY 1982-MARCH 1984)

Meanwhile, Ruhollah Musavi Khomeini aimed for a total defeat of Saddam Hussein's regime. Iran therefore launched a mammoth operation aiming to defeat the army of the Iraqi president and get to the heart of Iraq. The objective was to take possession of the city of Basra (second city) and the Faw peninsula, the gateway to the very strategic Shatt al-Arab. This mission, called Operation Ramadan, launched a wave of attacks in July 1982, with about 180 000 Iranians penetrating Iraqi territory, making this the largest ground offensive to fight since World War II (1939-1945).

Despite the resources committed, the operation was a failure. The lack of Iranian logistics and the superiority of the Iraqi equipment allowed Saddam Hussein to stop the Iranians before they reached Basra. Ruhollah Musavi Khomeini succeeded only in conquering 81 km^2 at the cost of thousands of lives. In the months that followed, he tried several times to reach the strategic Basra-Baghdad axis, without ever fully achieving it.

Nevertheless, Iran appealed to its very numerous infantry in the offensive of the Hawizeh marshes. Once again, the army of the Islamic Republic suffered heavy losses, but still managed to get hold of the Majnoon Islands and their oil.

PHASE 5: OIL IN SIGHT (APRIL 1984-JANUARY 1986)

Following the failure of the Iranian infantry, the front lines stabilized. Alongside this new stalemate, the two sides intensified their attacks on economic interests. Aided by French missiles, the Iraqis re-launched the bombardment of Iranian oil fields and the raids against the oil terminal of Kharg, the largest oil exporter to the Islamic Republic. Iran responded with strikes against ships serving Kuwaiti and Saudi ports, then allied with Iraq.

PHASE 6: THE WEST TO THE RESCUE OF IRAQ (FEBRUARY 1986-JANUARY 1988)

From February 1986, the Iranian army resumed its ground attacks and broke the status quo. It took the Faw peninsula, then, with the Iraqi Kurds, invaded part of Iraqi Kurdistan. The Iranian offensive then continued and in January 1987, took control of the Basra region.

Saddam Hussein reacted by increasing the use of his aviation. While it recorded 20 011 missions for the entire year of 1985, the Iraqi Air Force recorded nearly 18 648 flights between 9 February and 25 March 1986. However, despite this effort, the attempt of reconquest by Iraq ended in failure.

At the same time, Iranian attacks against the oil tankers of Iraq's allies resulted Kuwait's request for support from the great powers. The United States, which refused at first, agreed to this request after Kuwait pretended to turn to the Soviet Union.

In the wake of these events, the UN voted in favor of a new cease-fire on 20 July 1987. But, again, the treaty was rejected by Iran, which was pursuing its maritime attacks in the Gulf against Kuwaiti and American ships.

Four days later, a Kuwaiti supertanker escorted by the U.S. headed towards a mine attributed to Iran. This was followed by a deployment of 60 American, British and French vessels in the region.

In October 1987, the U.S. Navy sank three Iranian oil tankers under the pretext that they had shot down one of their patrol helicopters. They also destroyed an oil platform in response to the missile launched by Iran against a supertanker.

PHASE 7: THE USE OF CHEMICAL WEAPONS (FEBRUARY-JUNE 1988)

Boasting an increasingly massive support from foreign powers, Iraq began the recovery of its lost territories. Between 16 and 18 April 1988, Iraq regained the Faw Peninsula through the increasingly systematic use of chemical weapons, despite the rulings of international justice. From 23 to 25 May, Iraq massively used this type of weaponry again, in order to regain the lands in the north, in the center and in the south. In June of that same year, it took back the Manjoon Island, once again having used toxic gases.

In addition, thanks to new long-range missiles delivered by his allies, Saddam Hussein was now able to directly affect Tehran and thus demoralize the civilian population.

PHASE 8: THE END OF THE FIGHTING (SUMMER 1988)

On 3 July 1988, the American cruiser USS Vincennes mistakenly shot down an Iranian civilian plane that was carrying 290 passengers. Following this incident, the Iranians, exhausted, were finally convinced of the unfailing collaboration of the Westerners with the Iraqi camp. Thus, given the recent major military setbacks and the Western presence in the Gulf, Ruhollah Musavi Khomeini finally accepted the UN peace proposal. The cease-fire took effect on 8 August 1988 and the fighting ceased 12 days later.

A VERY CONTROVERSIAL WAR

Hiding the chemical weapons

One of the biggest scandals of this war was the use of chemical weapons by Saddam Hussein, supported by the United States. In 1983, Iraq violated the Geneva Protocol of 1925 – which banned the use of such weapons – by using sarin gas and mustard gas on Iranian soldiers, but also on the Kurdish population in northern Iraq, then allied with Iran. Under pressure from the U.S., which is now known to have played a direct role in the chemical attacks on the Iranian troops, the international community failed to react too harshly at first. However, the terrifying images of the gassing of the Kurds of Halabja shocked the world and the governments' denial stance was no longer tenable. On 25 May 1987, the use of chemical weapons was condemned by the European Community and the United States.

Iranian soldier wearing a gas mask

The unclear role of the U.S. administration

Under the regime of the Shah, the Americans had made Iran an unwavering ally in the Gulf. However, the United States, which believed that the Islamic Revolution would be a good defense against Communist subversion, hoped to renew this partnership after Ruhollah Musavi Khomeini took power. However, the hostage taking of U.S. diplomats by Iranian students led them to reconsider their position. When war broke out, the United States decided to help Saddam Hussein in his attempt to defeat the Ayatollah. Nonetheless, this American aid would be marred by numerous controversies.

The first scandal that erupted was that of the Irangate which directly involved President Ronald Wilson Raegan (1911-2004). The press of the time revealed that, while it publicly supported the Iraq of Saddam Hussein, the U.S. government sold weapons to the troops of Ruhollah Musavi Khomeini in the shadows. This caused a major scandal and Washington was unable to prevent a major loss of credibility.

The murky game played by America in this war did not stop there. A second scandal erupted, concerning the manipulations carried out by the United States in the case of the USS Stark frigate affair, touched by Iraqi fire. Following this error, Washington organized a vast disinformation campaign aimed at accusing Iran. This operation caused the actual entry of the Americans into the conflict, who now held a pretext to retaliate against the oil interests in Iran.

USS Stark destroyed by Iraqi missiles.

However, the most serious scandal involving the White House was certainly their involvement in the use of chemical weapons by Saddam Hussein against the Iranian troops. Indeed, in the face of the horrors committed by these weapons, the United States had always denied any involvement in the use of such gases. Yet, it is now certain that they had knowledge of the action of Saddam Hussein, but even worse, that they helped to improve the effectiveness of these attacks by informing the Iraqi army about the locations of their target.

Finally, the latest scandal to tarnish the American intervention was that of the USS Vincennes on 3 July 1988. Mistaking an Iranian airliner for a unit of the Air Force, a U.S. ship, the USS Vincennes, shot at it, causing 290 Iranian civilian casualties. Once again, the United States tried to cover up the affair, claiming it was a suicide bomber plane. This disinformation campaign was once again a failure. However, feeling more and more pressure from the U.S. troops, Iran, cornered, decided to resign and sign the cease-fire proposed by the UN.

Saddam Hussein, a friend who would humiliate France

In order to nurture its industry after the Second World War, French President Charles de Gaulle (1890-1970) was careful to spare his Arab allies by criticizing the attacks by Israel against Egypt in June 1967 during the Six-Day War (5-10 June 1967). France quickly became the third provider to Iraq through the active role of Saddam Hussein, the real architect of the Franco-Iraqi agreement. In 1974, Paris signed many contracts with Baghdad, securing good economic and military cooperation between the two countries. It was in this context that negotiations were opened for the sale of two civilian nuclear reactors to Saddam Hussein. However, this transaction caused a stir because many people believed that Iraq sought above all to obtain nuclear weapons. This risk was also taken very seriously by Israel, who conducted the bombing of these facilities a few months later.

Thereafter, at the beginning of the Iran-Iraq War, France, who saw Iran as a great danger, intensified its arms shipments to Iraq. However, this cooperation with Saddam Hussein's regime led to France becoming the target of a wave of attacks that were associated with Iranian intelligence. Besides these assaults, close collaboration with Iraq was fast becoming uncomfortable for the French government, which would find it more and more difficult to justify this special relationship as the massacres perpetrated with chemical weapons by Saddam Hussein came to light.

The outcome of the fighting: all for nothing

After eight years of bloody conflict, the war ended with an unlikely status quo. There were no winners or losers. The two countries resumed the same borders as those of 1975, while Ruhollah Musavi Khomeini had to recognize the failure of his export of the Islamic Revolution to Iraq. However, in this outcome that ultimately solved nothing, it was the people who had suffered the most. This war was indeed one of the most destructive and deadly of the 20th century.

In terms of human losses:

- In Iran, there were, according to official figures, 194 931 deaths, including 183 931 military losses and 11 000 civilian losses. However, estimates often indicate a range of 220 000 to 400 000 deaths;
- In Iraq, the estimated losses were between 200 000 and 500 000 men.

Economically, the war cost:

- For Iran, between 74 and 91 billion dollars and 11.26 billion dollars of military imports, according to estimates;
- For Iraq, between 94 and 112 billion dollars and 41.94 billion dollars of military imports, according to estimates.

REPERCUSSIONS OF THE WAR

On the evening of 20 August 1988, noting that the two countries had returned to their pre-war borders, but mostly that none of the sources of tension had been solved, the general feeling was that the war had been a huge mess. The conflict was the scene of an incredible waste of human lives and material resources, eventually leading to a standstill. Yet, historical perspective allows us to observe that these eight years of conflict were not without consequence.

TWO CONSOLIDATED REGIMES

Safeguarding the Islamic Republic

Against all expectations, the war had, at first, undermined neither of the belligerent regimes. Paradoxically, the hardship and the durability of the fighting allowed Ruhollah Musavi Khomeini to consolidate his Islamic revolution. While still in its infancy and beset by many quarrels in 1980, the Republic established by the Ayatollah was able to federate the Iranian people in a block surrounding the supreme leader and his army against the hereditary enemy: the Sunni Arabs. Moreover, this war helped to mask the many problems of economic management of the Islamic government.

An increasingly dictatorial power

With an army that counted a million men and a large stock of modern weapons supplied by the Soviet Union and the West, Iraq was now among the major powers in the region.

Moreover, this war allowed Saddam Hussein to significantly strengthen his personal power. Heading further and further towards despotism, the president took advantage of the conflict to proceed to the elimination of all opposition. He thus proceeded to massacre the Iraqi Shiites in the south who favored the Islamic Republic, but also to eliminate the Kurdish rebels fighting alongside Iran. This policy of radical suppression of the opposition led Saddam Hussein, on Sunday 16 March 1988, to carry out the gassing of the Kurdish population of Halabja, in complete violation of all international conventions on the use of chemical weapons.

THE TIME FOR QUESTIONING

A somewhat liberating death

However, the consolidation of the two regimes only lasted for a time. As the months passed, the wounds of war were beginning to re-open. In Iran, the image of Ruhollah Musavi Khomeini – and therefore of Islamic power – was tarred when he ordered the mass elimination of the prisoners of war. Within months, the authority carried out the execution of more than 30 000 prisoners. This bloodbath did not leave people insensitive. The alleged successor of Ruhollah Musavi Khomeini, Ayatollah Montazeri (1922-2009), at the risk of violent reprisals, began protesting against the massacre himself. He would be removed from power following his criticism.

In addition, Ruhollah Musavi Khomeini died on 3 June 1989, and though mourned by millions of followers, this allowed for some questioning of the exercise of power by the Ayatollah. However, this was not a massive revolt against the late supreme leader, but quite the opposite. Nonetheless, after his death, some began to show their disagreement with his policy of abstention during the war, as well as his lack of vision regarding the practical management of internal affairs. Meanwhile, others were hoping for a more moderate regime on the part of his successor Hossein Ali Khamenei (born in 1939).

Ali Khamenei, 2006.

Too much provocation

When the fighting ceased in 1988, Iraq was economically devastated. Faced with its debts, Saddam Hussein asked Kuwait to cancel Iraq's debt, amounting to several billion dollars. When Kuwait refused, Saddam Hussein took a gamble: invading its rich neighbor and getting hold of its many oil resources, right under the nose of the international community, which had been particularly accommodating towards him until then.

However, after the invasion, the international community, to which Iraq was also heavily indebted, did not remain inactive and voted for the introduction of stringent economic sanctions to try to bring Saddam Hussein to reason. Nonetheless, this blockade which could strengthen the financial distress of Iraq did not have the desired effect. Radicalized, Saddam Hussein refused the ultimatum and continued his invasion.

On 17 January 1991, deciding to react, the American President George Herbert Walker Bush took the lead of a coalition of 34 countries and attacked the Iraqi forces. Faced with the international fire power, Saddam Hussein's attempt turned into a disaster. Within days, his army was swept up and had to withdraw from Kuwait. The consequences for him would be dramatic. The operation caused a complete disavowal of Iraq by the international community, while economic sanctions introduced by the latter prompted a catastrophic fall in the living conditions of the Iraqis. Saddam Hussein went from an enlightened despot to a tyrant in the eyes of the world, eventually being overthrown and executed on 30 December 2006, following the attack on Iraq by the United States of George W. Bush Jr. and his allies.

Saddam Hussein shortly after his capture, December 2003.

SUMMARY

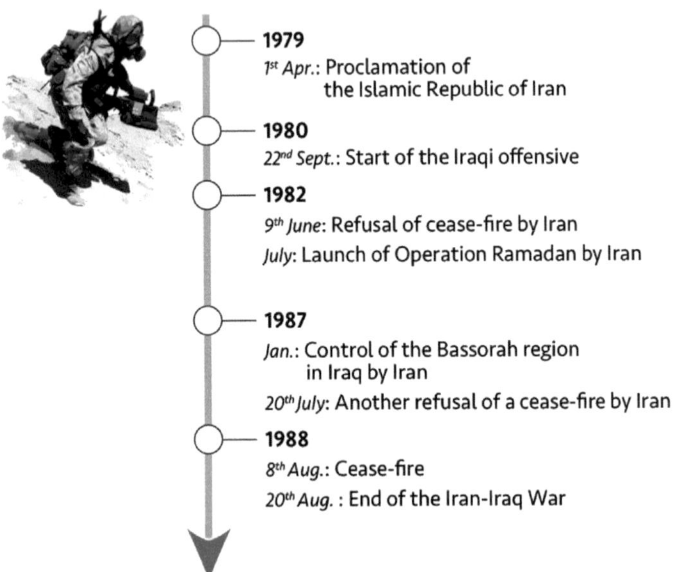

- Saddam Hussein wished to make the Republic of Iraq an indispensable power in his region of the globe.
- Ayatollah Ruhollah Musavi Khomeini planned to export his Islamic Revolution beyond the borders of Iran and extend it to the Iraqis.
- In 1980, both sides multiplied provocations around their border area of the Shatt al-Arab River, thus violating the territorial treaty signed in Algiers in 1975.
- On 22 September 1980, Saddam Hussein launched all of his forces on Iran.
- The Iraqi offensive galvanized the Iranians who gathered

around Ruhollah Musavi Khomeini and pushed them to engage massively in the conflict.
- Contrary to Iraqi estimates, the conflict quickly became bogged down.
- Following the successive refusals of peace talks by Iran, the West offered increasing support to Iraq.
- From the beginning of 1988, despite international law, Saddam Hussein intensified the use of chemical weapons to regain the territories taken by Iran.
- On 20 July 1988, exhausted and now convinced by the unwavering support of the United States to Iraq, Iran finally agreed to the UN peace proposal.
- This war lasted nearly eight years, ultimately ending in a paltry territorial status quo.
- The human and economic losses were appalling, making this one of the most devastating conflicts since World War II.
- Despite this huge mess, the war allowed Saddam Hussein and Ruhollah Musavi Khomeini to silence internal opposition and consolidate their respective regimes.
- The horror caused by the use of chemical weapons on populations (particularly the Kurds in Halabja) caused Westerners to disengage definitively from Saddam Hussein, who would be executed in 2006 following the attack on Iraq by the United States.

FIND OUT MORE

BIBLIOGRAPHY

- Balta, P. (1999) *Iran-Irak. Une guerre de 5 000 ans.* Paris: Anthropos.
- Gardner, A.J. (1988) *The Iraq-Iran War: A Bibliography.* London: Mansell.
- Cordesman, A.H. (1988) *The Gulf and the West: Strategic Relations and Military Realities.* London: Mansell.
- Fisk, R. (2006) *The Great War for Civilisation: The Conquest of the Middle East.* London: Harper Perennial.
- Hiro, D. (1989) *The Longest War. The Iran-Iraq Military Conflict.* London: Grafton.
- Hiro, D. (1996) *Dictionary of the Middle East.* London: Macmillian.
- Hourcade, B. (2010) *Géopolitique de l'Iran.* Paris: Armand Colin.
- Tahir-Kheli, S. and Ayubi, S. (1983) *The Iran-Iraq War: New Weapons, Old Conflicts.* New York: Praeger.
- Tameri, A. and Wajsman, P. (2002) *Irak. Le dessous des cartes.* Brussels: Complexe.

ADDITIONAL SOURCES

- Menashri, D. (1990) *Iran: A Decade of War and Revolution.* New York: Holmes & Meier.
- Miller, J. and Mylroie, L. (1990) *Saddam Hussein and the Crisis in the Gulf.* New York: Ballantine Books.
- Trab Zemzemi, A.M. (1986) *The Iran-Iraq War: Islam and Nationalisms.* USA: United States Publishing Co.

ICONOGRAPHIC SOURCES

- Poster of the Iranian Revolution showing the Shah taking refuge in the USA, 1979. © "Groupe 57", a Leftist student group in Iran.
- Destruction of a statue of the Shah Mohammad Reza Pahlavi, February 1979. Royalty-free reproduction picture.
- Ruhollah Khomeini, 1979. Royalty-free reproduction picture.
- Poster of the Islamic Republic against Saddam Hussein's regime. Imam Khomeini. © Jean-Pierre Dalbéra.
- Saddam Hussein, 1979. © INA (Iraqi News Agency).
- Battle of Khorramshahr (Iran), from 22 September to 10 November 1980. Royalty-free reproduction picture.
- Iranian soldier wearing a gas mask. Royalty-free reproduction picture.
- USS Stark destroyed by Iraqi missiles. Royalty-free reproduction picture.
- Ali Khamenei, 2006. © Seyyed Shabodin Vajedi.
- Saddam Hussein shortly after his capture, December 2003. Royalty-free reproduction picture.

LITERATURE

- Powers, K. (2012) *The Yellow Birds*. New York: Little, Brown and Company.
- Satrapi, M. (2008) *Persepolis*. London: Vintage.

FILMS AND DOCUMENTARIES

- *Iran-Irak : la guerre totale.* (1988) [Documentary]. Gilles Du Jonchay. Dir. France.
- Bashu, gharibeye koochak. (1989) [Film]. Bahram Beizai. Dir. Iran: The Institute for the Intellectual Development of Children and Young Adults.
- *Az Karkheh ta Rhein.* (1993) [Film]. Ebrahim Hatamikia. Dir. Iran.
- *Gilane.* (2005) [Film]. Rakhshan Bani Etemad and Mohsen Abdel Wahab. Dir. Iran: Fadak Film.

MUSEUMS AND COMMEMORATIVE BUILDINGS

- Cemetery of the Martyrs of the Sacred Defense in Howeyzeh (Iran).
- Mausoleum of the Ayatollah Ruhollah Musavi Khomeini in Tehran (Iran).
- The memorial commemorating the massacre with chemical weapons of the Kurds of Halabja (Kurdistan).
- The Tehran Peace Memorial dedicated to the victims of chemical weapons in the city of Sardasht (Iran).
- The Al-Shaheed Monument in Baghdad dedicated to the fallen Iraqi soldiers during the war (Iraq).
- The Museum of Sacred Defense in Khorramshahr (Iran).
- The Victory Arch in Baghdad celebrating the alleged victory of Iraq during the war (Iraq).

IMPROVE YOUR GENERAL KNOWLEDGE

IN A BLINK OF AN EYE !

www.50minutes.com

www.50minutes.com

Ebook EAN: 9782806273208

Paperback EAN: 9782806273215

Legal Deposit: D/2015/12603/643

Cover: © Primento

Digital conception by Primento, the digital partner of publishers.